LIFEHOUSE
NO NAME FACE

CONTENTS

FRONT COVER: "THE CHAPERONE" BY MAXFIELD PARRISH
PHOTO COURTESY OF THE ARCHIVES OF
THE AMERICAN ILLUSTRATORS GALLERY, NEW YORK CITY
©2001 ASaP, NEW HAMPSHIRE, USA

ISBN 1-57560-450-7

Copyright © 2001 Cherry Lane Music Company
International Copyright Secured   All Rights Reserved

The music, text, design and graphics in this publication are protected by copyright law.
Any duplication or transmission, by any means, electronic, mechanical, photocopying,
recording or otherwise, is an infringement of copyright.

Visit our website at www.cherrylane.com

LIFEHOUSE

JASON WADE: VOCALS, GUITAR
SERGIO ANDRADE: BASS
RICK WOOLSTENHULME: DRUMS

"I don't have it all figured out," says Lifehouse singer-guitarist-songwriter Jason Wade. "You learn so many things every day, and it's overwhelming sometimes trying to see how it all fits together. I'm starting to realize that each day is a different road and a different journey, and you don't have to have it all figured out; you don't *have* to have all the answers to everything right now."

One of the things Jason hasn't figured out is how Lifehouse went from playing a few college shows to sharing the road with Pearl Jam, Fuel, Everclear, and matchbox twenty.

Perhaps even more incomprehensible is how this recently obscure Los Angeles band scored a #1 hit on *Billboard*'s Modern Rock Tracks chart ("Hanging by a Moment") only ten weeks after the release of their debut album, *No Name Face*. Jason, Sergio, and Rick were equally incredulous at the appearance of their song "Everything" on the popular TV show *Roswell*.

"It's all been unbelievable," Jason says of Lifehouse's success thus far. "We didn't expect any of this, but we're so grateful to have so many people hearing our songs. I really can't explain how it's happened."

In fact, the trio's frontman is hard-pressed to explain most of the unexpected twists his life has taken. His early years in Camarillo, California, for instance, would suggest an all-American boyhood, but then his family began touring the Far East, visiting Japan, Thailand, and Singapore before moving to Hong Kong. Moreover, he admits to having little interest in music until his parents split up and the songs just started pouring out of him.

"This record deals a lot with self-discovery and breaking out of whatever your parents or your boss or whoever thinks you should be," says Jason of *No Name Face*. "It's about trying to find out for yourself who you're supposed to be—your purpose, your destiny in the world."

Reluctant to discuss his lyrics in detail, Jason feels they are infinitely open to interpretation. "That's the great thing about a song—a lyric may mean something totally different for someone else than it does for me and still be just as valid," he insists. A case in point is album closer, "Everything": "We've been playing it on tour and when kids come up after the show, it seems like they always tell us how much they love that song. They don't really know what it's about, but they hear something in it that connects to them personally. That's why you don't have to tell the whole picture in the lyrics; you give a road to start on that people can relate to."

Jason understands firsthand how bleak life can seem without something or someone to relate to. "When I was a kid and we lived in Hong Kong, we lived in a small village and the people there hated us," he says. "They thought we were witches bringing trouble to their neighborhood. They lit firecrackers at our door every morning, and they actually stole our cat, cooked and ate it! I was totally scared and freaked out and I didn't have any friends."

After four difficult years, Jason's family moved back to the U.S., to Portland, Oregon. Asked why, he ventures: "My parents had a lot of issues. But they wouldn't allow me to see the problems in their relationship. Our family was always peaceful; there was never any fighting or anything. We looked perfectly happy from the outside. It was like 'Pleasantville.' The worst part was that I couldn't acknowledge anything was wrong, so I couldn't do anything about it. I felt completely powerless."

By the time he was 12, Jason's parents had divorced and he'd moved with his mom to the Seattle area. He spent most of his early days there alone in his room, pouring his heart out in poetry. "I was experiencing all the pain anyone feels when their parents get divorced. It opened up all this stuff," he confides. "But it also opened up this creative outlet for me. It's funny, because I was never a musical kid—never took lessons, never really listened to the radio. But I suddenly just started writing lyrics and coming up with melodies. We lived in the woods, and I'd take these long walks and the songs would just start happening."

Jason's mother *had* been musical. "My mom always had a guitar lying around the house," he recollects. "I finally just picked it up and learned how to play a few chords." Having found some solace in music, he eventually began reconciling himself to his new circumstances and settled into his new home.

This phase of his life ended, however, when his mother decided to relocate the family to Los Angeles. "I didn't want to move at all," he attests. "I'd finally made all these friends, and Washington had been a really comforting place for me during the divorce. I thought it would be home forever."

So, at 15, Jason moved to L.A., where he hooked up with bassist Sergio Andrade and began blossoming as a songwriter. "I really didn't know anyone. Serge lived next door and we had a lot of stuff in common, like playing basketball and running," he says. "He'd just started playing bass, so we hung out a lot. We spent all our time jamming out in the garage, writing songs and helping each other get better."

Originally from Guatemala City, Sergio left his homeland at age 14 to move to California. He, too, had a musical parent. "My father played piano," he confirms, "and I ended up playing keyboards." He gravitated toward rock, pop, and Latin styles, also playing trombone and flute in the school orchestra.

Sergio later switched to drums and then bass, becoming somewhat obsessed with the instrument—"All I did was play bass," he says. "I knew Jason was a talented guy, but that wasn't what mattered to me," Sergio continues. "I was still learning English and really didn't know anyone. I just wanted to be involved in music and make some friends."

The two paired with a drummer (who has since left the group) and after honing their sound for a few more months, inaugurated a Friday night residency at a local school auditorium. The gatherings were casual events where the band was afforded onstage jam time (some of these jams became songs, among them "Everything"). "They had a really good P.A. system there and we could do whatever we wanted," Jason reports. "We got smoke machines and lights and basically turned it into this little club scene. Kids would come from all over, and we started filling the place up. At one point we were getting, like, 450 people out every week. That went on for two years."

Word of mouth about the band soon reached *No Name Face* producer Ron Aniello, who let them make some rudimentary recordings at his home studio.

Drummer Rick Woolstenhulme also heard about the band through the grapevine. Born and raised in the Arizona farm town of Gilbert, he says he was one of those kids who was always pounding on things. "My mom plays piano, my dad plays piano and guitar, and my brother plays guitar," Rick relates. "I guess they decided I was the next musician in the family, so they got me this beat-up old kit and I started taking lessons right away." Rick went on to attend the Los Angeles Music Academy and has played drums and percussion ever since.

"I was playing with this other group," he says of his earliest, accidental exposure to Lifehouse, "and Jason and Serge were practicing in the next room—I'd bump into them in the hallway." A while later, someone suggested to Rick that he check out a band called Lifehouse, who were looking for a new drummer. "The name didn't ring a bell for me. Even after I officially met these guys, we didn't make the connection right away," he recalls. "It was a couple weeks of 'I've seen you somewhere' and 'you look really familiar' before we figured it out."

Remarks Jason, "It was one of those weird coincidences. As soon as we met and started playing with Rick we knew he was the guy. It just clicked. We'd all go to the beach and Burger King and just do nothing together. We knew right away it was going to work." Attests Rick, "It was really smooth; I just sort of snapped on."

Sergio says of the band's collaboration, "Jason would usually have the song written before he'd bring it to us. Then we'd all kind of arrange it together. The way we work on songs feels really natural, which I think has a lot to do with us being tight as a band and as friends."

Aniello saw the progress Lifehouse was making but felt the band needed more time to develop before recording an album. So Jason kept on writing, and the trio continued to rehearse intensively and play gigs, including some at local colleges. Comments

Sergio, "We went through a lot of phases trying to find our own sound. We learned from our mistakes. We'd see tapes of ourselves onstage and go, 'This is horrible.' But we'd just say, 'Okay, we gotta fix it,' and go back and practice some more.

"Jason stayed in touch with Aniello. Two years passed, and then he played "Breathing" for the producer. "He got really excited about it," Jason says, "and he played it for his friend Jude Cole, who's our manager now.

"I was blown away by what I heard," says Cole. "Here were these teenagers skateboarding around their tract-house neighborhood and banging out this really deep music in the garage. I was totally moved by 'Breathing'—it was the kind of song that captures a moment in time, the kind you always remember where you were when you first heard it. Jason was only 17, but he already had that incredibly resonant voice. I was also impressed by his writing and guitar work. He had an instinctive understanding of how to create a mood. Even before Ron started playing me their other stuff, I knew I had to work with this band."

Cole immediately called DreamWorks Records principal Michael Ostin, who had been Cole's own A&R representative when Cole was a recording artist. In 1998, DreamWorks funded Lifehouse's first real demos, which Aniello produced.

Many of these tracks made their way to *No Name Face.* "When we tried to re-record some of the songs for the album, we just couldn't get the same spirit the demos had," Jason says. "The demos had been recorded right after the songs were written and even though they weren't perfect, they were so real, so honest." "Trying," for instance, is fundamentally the same recording Jason made at Ron's home studio when he was 15, with one significant change: "I had to go back in and re-record my vocals for the album because my voice had changed."

The rest of *No Name Face* was also laid down mostly at Aniello's home studio. "Ron's studio is right down the street from us," Jason says. "If we'd been working really late, we'd just spend the night there. We'd wake up, have breakfast with Ron and get right back to it. He's been like a father to me in a lot of ways, and the whole recording process had this homegrown, family feel that made it so easy to be creative. I wrote

'Hanging by a Moment' in the studio while we were finishing some other stuff."

Jason's trust in Aniello helped make these sessions a learning experience. "I came in wanting it to be all slick and fancy," he concedes. "I was so excited to be in the studio making a record—I wanted every instrument and every effect on the planet. Ron said pretty early that he felt the record should sound organic, that the production should be simple and transparent. I'd have all these ideas, and we did use some of them, but after a while I realized he was right. The record needed to sound more raw."

This sonic edge was indeed the right complement to Lifehouse's emotionally charged songs. Evidence of that can be found in the thousands of calls placed to Modern Rock stations across America requesting "Hanging by a Moment."

"The best thing about all this is being able to stay on the road," says Jason. "We've been meeting new fans in cities all over the country. It's so cool to hear what they think about the music, and it makes me feel so good when they say that one of our songs has helped them get through a rough time, that they were able to apply it to their own life."

To be sure, this is the sort of opportunity only afforded a band on the way up. But Jason and his mates have had no trouble staying grounded amid all the hubbub. After all, it's not like they've actually *met* Pearl Jam. "We love Pearl Jam," Jason says. "Once we got over the shock of actually being on tour with them, we went backstage to hang out with them. But security would never let us through the door. We tried a bunch of times and could never get in. I'm sure the band didn't even know about it. And, of course, security had no idea who we were—we were just some fans."

Being "just a fan," a music lover like any other, is what Jason is and always wants to be. "My ultimate goal in writing songs is simply to connect with people," he says, "and I hope that comes across in everything we do."

ABOUT THE SONGS
BY JASON WADE

HANGING BY A MOMENT
This is a love song that can be interpreted in a bunch of different ways.

SICK CYCLE CAROUSEL
It's about my relationship with my girlfriend. There was a specific time when we felt the struggles of going through a relationship, of trying to communicate and going through all the things you go through to get to that point of real depth. I wrote the song during the most crucial time— when we were either going to break up, or continue our relationship.

UNKNOWN
I wrote that with [manager] Jude Cole and [producer] Ron Aniello. I wasn't planning on co-writing with anyone, but Jude had the chorus— "I am falling into grace/ To the unknown to where you are/ And faith makes everybody scared/ It's the unknown, the don't-know/ That keeps me hanging onto you." I really connected to it and it totally fit in with my other lyrics. I wrote the verses to it and the bridge and it all just went together. I like writing with other people now. It depends on the mood I'm in, though. Most of the time I write by myself, but if the mood's right, it's fun to collaborate.

SOMEBODY ELSE'S SONG
When I was writing "Somebody Else's Song" I had this picture of some kid with all these expectations on him, about what he's supposed to become in the world and what he's supposed to do. That's where I got that lyric "I got somebody else's thoughts in my head/ I want some of my own/ I want some of my own." It's about figuring things out for yourself. There was this whole period where I was searching and trying to think for myself. I was, like, I don't want to believe in something just because my parents believe in it. Or, I don't want to go to college just because they told me to go to college. I think people go through that kind of stuff their whole lives.

TRYING
I wrote "Trying" when I was 15. It's about the same kind of spiritual searching as "Only One." After my parents got divorced, I wrote the lyrics to it, then learned how to play guitar and came up with the melody. The song's about finding your way in life. I was trying to figure out what I wanted to do, what I wanted to become, not just in music but also who I was as a person. I consider "Trying" my first song, the first one I didn't scrap. The funny thing is, I can relate to it more now than I could back then. Sometimes I think, "Man—where did that come from?" I still feel the same emotion when I play it, so I guess it's pretty timeless; people can relate to it, no matter how old they are.

ONLY ONE
I wrote "Only One" right after someone in my life did something I felt was totally wrong. It was a really tough time for me. I have these trails in my life, like my dad leaving and my not being with him anymore, and then this man, who I really looked up to, failing. "Only One" is about how sometimes people are just not there for you and you have to look

SIMON

I wrote this about a friend of mine who told me about his childhood. He was telling me how he went to school and was the outcast and everyone picked on him and called him names, and he didn't have one friend. I started feeling the same emotions he must have felt and just started writing these lyrics. I think some of the stuff from [growing up in] Hong Kong might have been related to that, not having any friends at that age and being, as a family, the outcast in a different culture. The feeling of being alone, of being abandoned, connects to that. So "Simon" came really easily—I wrote it in about 15 minutes. These lyrics just poured out and I wrote them down and recorded it on the spot.

CLING AND CLATTER

That's about trying to make your way through the cling and clatter— all the noise and emotional distractions—to get to what you really need. It's about sorting through the conflicting voices inside and outside your head.

BREATHING

This is another love song that can be interpreted in a couple of different ways. The verses say, "I'm finding my way back to sanity again." So it's like trying really hard and then getting back to the place you started from. Then the bridge says "I don't want a thing from you/ Bet you're tired of me waiting for the scraps to fall off of your table to the ground." It's kind of like not wanting anything from anyone, not hanging on every word they say and just having faith you'll be able to "be here now," which is how the song ends.

QUASIMODO

"Quasimodo" is a character who's chained down by people trying to get him to conform. Sometimes I get pictures of people when I'm writing. I look at this person like some kid at school who doesn't look as cool as the rest of the kids and doesn't act as cool. There's a group of kids that come along and try to make him what they want him to be and do things he doesn't want to do. He goes along with it 'cause he's afraid. But by the chorus, he's breaking out of that, saying, "There goes my pain/ There goes my chains/ Did you see them fall/ There goes this feeling that has no meaning/ There goes the world/ Off of my shoulders." So it ends hopefully.

SOMEWHERE IN BETWEEN

Before my girlfriend and I got together, she had broken up with this guy. I'd been head-over-heels for her for years even though she was dating him. So they broke up, and I was like, "Man, if I don't make a move now, I may never get a chance." I was always friends with her but never really could get a step further. So I started taking her out to dinners and stuff. She was a little bit on the rebound, but I think she had some feelings for me. We were at that point where we weren't sure if we were dating or not, or even if she really liked me in that way. It was a very vulnerable time for me and that's when I wrote "Somewhere In Between." I poured all those feelings into the song. Then I played it for her and that was it—we were together.

EVERYTHING

That's a super-special song for me. It seems to really connect with other people, too. It's one of those songs that every time I played it, a new part came to it. That's why it's so long and kind of mysterious. It's a bunch of different bits and pieces, but it has power because it kind of sums up everything I'm about—lyrically and in terms of my relationships and Lifehouse overall. So I think it's a perfect way to end the record.

HANGING BY A MOMENT

Words and Music by
Jason Wade

Drop D tuning, tune down 1/2 step:
low to high (D♭-A♭-D♭-G♭-B♭-E♭)

Intro

Moderate Rock ♩ = 124

*D

Gtr. 1 (clean)   Riff A

mf let ring throughout

*Chord symbols reflect implied harmony.

End Riff A

Verse

D

1. Des - p'rate____ for____ chang - ing,_____ starv - ing____ for____ truth.____

Riff A1

Copyright © 2000 Songs Of DreamWorks (BMI) and G Chills Music (BMI)
Worldwide Rights for Songs Of Dreamworks and G Chills Music Administered by Cherry River Music Co.
International Copyright Secured All Rights Reserved

End Riff A1

I'm clos - er to where I start - ed,_____ oh,

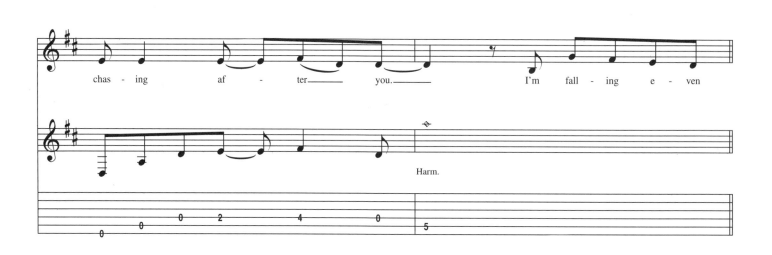

chas - ing af - ter_____ you._____ I'm fall - ing e - ven

Harm.

Chorus

Bm   A   D   Bm   A   D

more in love___ with you,_____ let - ting go of all I've held___ on to._____ I'm stand - ing here un -

Gtr. 2 (clean)

mf

Gtr. 1

Interlude

2. For -

Verse

I'll take your in - vi - ta - tion.

You take all___ of me,___ now. I'm fall - ing e - ven

more in love___ with you,___ let - ting go of all I've held___ on to.___

*Bass plays F#.

I'm stay-ing here un-til you make— me move.— I'm hang-ing by a

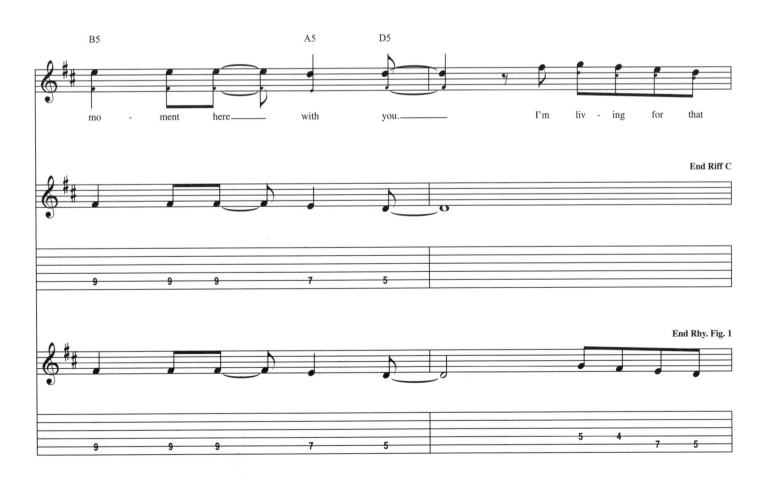

mo - ment here— with you.— I'm liv - ing for that

End Riff C

End Rhy. Fig. 1

Gtr. 1: w/ Riff C
Gtr. 2: w/ Rhy. Fig. 1 (1st 7 meas.)
2nd time, Gtr. 2: w/ Rhy. Fig. 1

on - ly thing— I know.— I'm run-ning and not quite sure where— to go.—

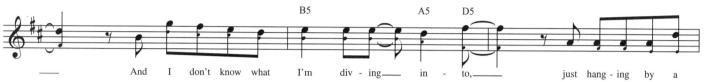

— And I don't know what I'm div-ing— in-to,— just hang-ing by a

1st time, Gtr. 2: w/ Fill 1

To Coda ✛

mo - ment here— with you.— { There's noth-ing else— to lose,—
Just hang - ing by a

Bridge

— there's noth-ing else— to find.—

Gtrs. 1 & 2

There's noth-ing in the world that can change my

Fill 1
Gtr. 2

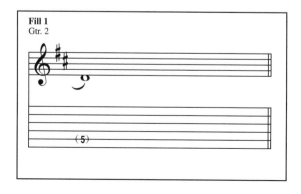

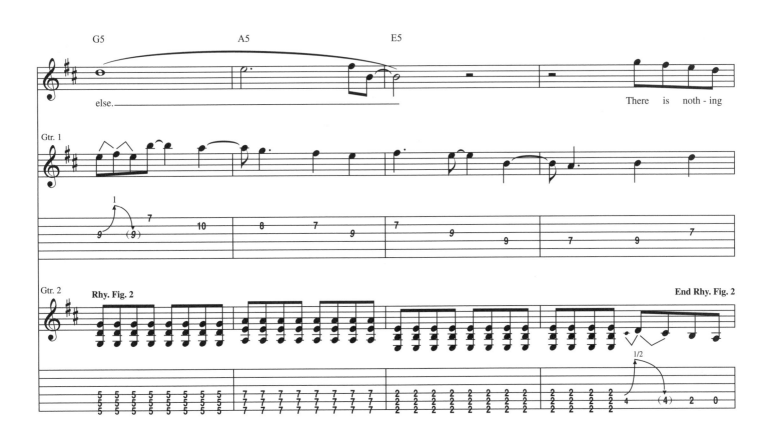

else.

Interlude

w/ clean tone
let ring -

*w/ clean tone

Verse

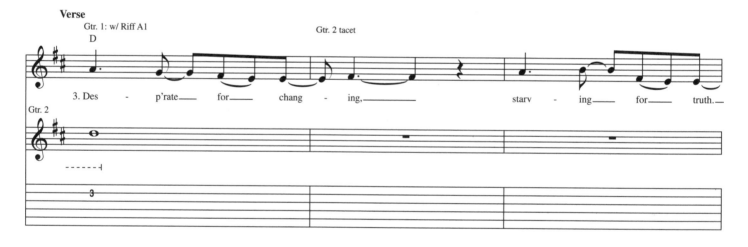

3. Des - p'rate___ for___ chang - ing,___ starv - ing___ for___ truth.___

___ I'm clos - er to where I start - ed,___ oh,

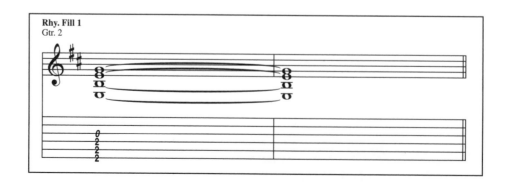

Rhy. Fill 1
Gtr. 2

chas - ing af - ter____ you.____ I'm fall - ing e - ven

Gtr. 1

let ring - Harm.

⊕ **Coda**
Outro-Chorus

Gtr. 1: w/ Riff C (1st 6 meas.)
Gtr. 2: w/ Rhy. Fig. 1 (1st 6 meas.)

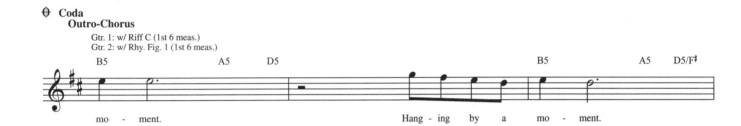

B5   A5 D5   B5   A5 D5/F♯

mo - ment.   Hang - ing by a mo - ment.

B5   A5 D5

Hang - ing by a mo - ment.   Hang - ing by a

B5   A5 D5

mo - ment here____ with   you.____

Gtr. 1

Gtr. 2

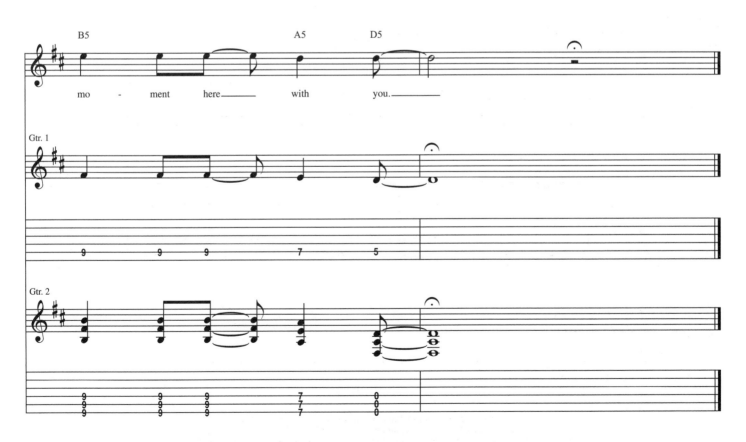

SICK CYCLE CAROUSEL

Words and Music by
Jason Wade and Scott Faircloff

Copyright © 2000 Songs Of DreamWorks (BMI), G Chills Music (BMI),
Pamplin Music Publishing (ASCAP) and Rifferous Music (ASCAP)/both admin. by ICG
Worldwide Rights for Songs Of Dreamworks and G Chills Music Administered by Cherry River Music Co.
International Copyright Secured   All Rights Reserved

* Symbols in parentheses represent chord names respective to capoed guitar.
Symbols above reflect actual sounding chords. Capoed fret is "0" in tab.

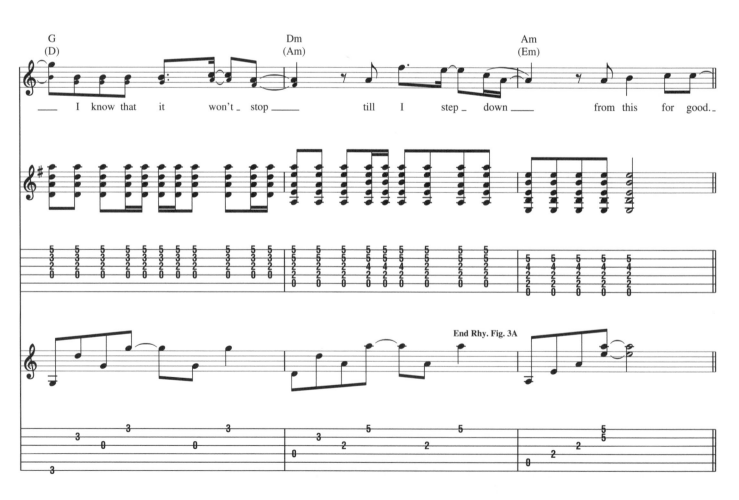

Gtr. 5: w/ Riff C (2 times)

Am   Em   F   C   G/B

— I tried — to see how low ___ I could get ___ down to the ground. ___ And,

Am   Em   F   C   G/B

well, I tried — to earn my ___ way. ___ I tried — to change this ___ mind. ___

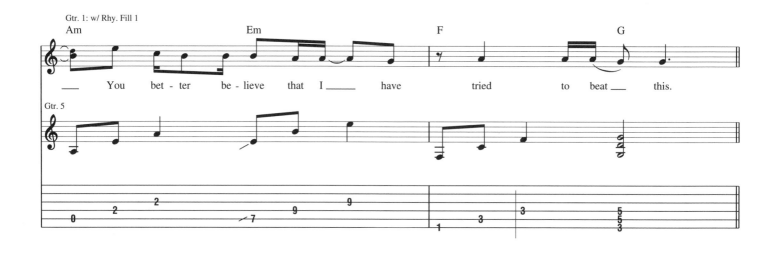

Gtr. 1: w/ Rhy. Fill 1

Am   Em   F   G

— You bet-ter be-lieve that I ___ have tried to beat ___ this.

Gtr. 5

Chorus

Gtr. 1: w/ Rhy. Fig. 3 (1 3/4 times)
Gtr. 2: w/ Fill 1
Gtr. 3: w/ Rhy. Fig. 3A
Gtr. 5 tacet

Csus2   G
(G)   (D)

So when will this ___ end? ___ It goes on and on, ___

Gtr. 6   Riff D

w/ slide

Gtr. 4

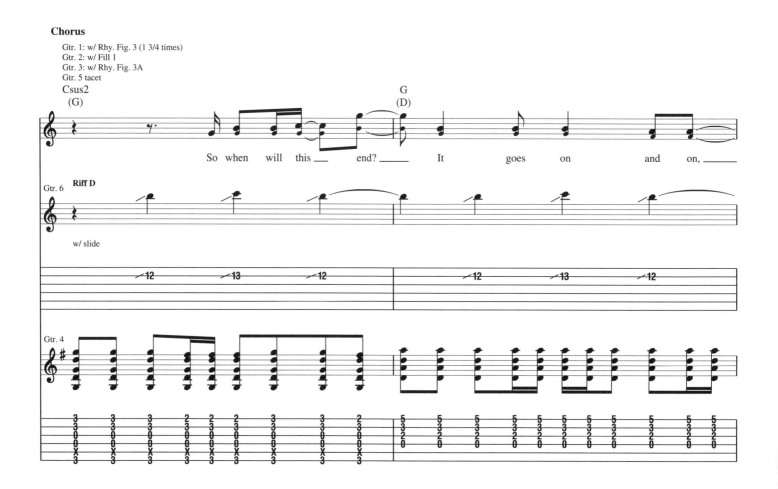

Chorus

So when will this __ end? __ It goes on and on, __ o - ver and o - ver and o - ver a - gain.

Riff E　　　　　　　　　　　　　　　　　**End Riff E**

Gtr. 4: w/ Riff E (3 times)

__ Keep spin - ning a - round, __ I know that it won't __ stop __ till I step __ down __

Gtr. 6: w/ Riff D (2 times)

__ from this for good. __ Where will this __ end? __ It goes on and on, __

__ o - ver and o - ver and o - ver a - gain. __ Keep spin - ning a - round, __

__ I know that it won't __ stop __ till I step __ down __ from this for good. __

Outro

Repeat and fade

Gtrs. 1 & 3: w/ Rhy. Fig. 3 (till end)
Gtrs. 4 & 6: w/ Riffs D & E (till end)
Lead Voc.: ad lib on repeats

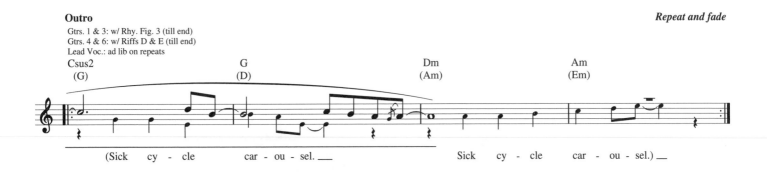

(Sick cy - cle car - ou - sel. __ Sick cy - cle car - ou - sel.) __

UNKNOWN

Words and Music by Jason Wade,
Ron Aniello and Jude Cole

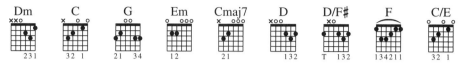

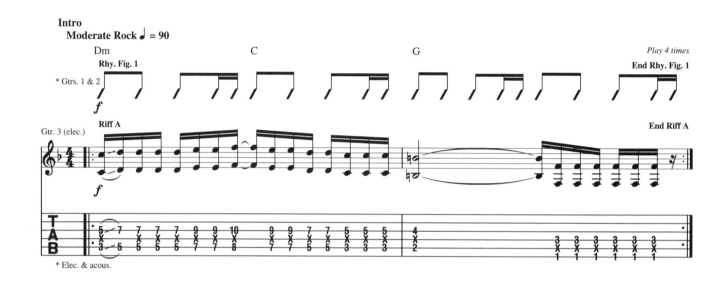

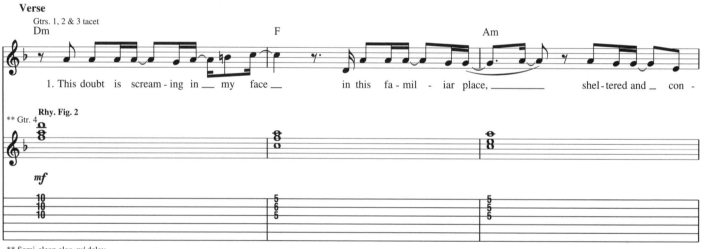

Copyright © 2000 Songs Of DreamWorks (BMI), G Chills Music (BMI), EMI Blackwood Music Inc. (BMI), Aniello Music (BMI),
Warner-Tamerlane Publishing Corp. (BMI) and Jude Cole Music (BMI)
Worldwide Rights for Songs Of Dreamworks and G Chills Music Administered by Cherry River Music Co.
Worldwide Rights for Aniello Music Controlled and Administered by EMI Blackwood Music Inc.
International Copyright Secured   All Rights Reserved

Interlude

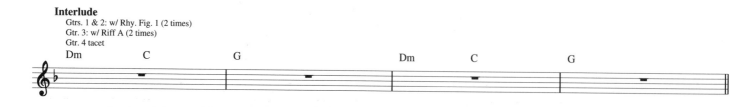

SOMEBODY ELSE'S SONG

Words and Music by
Jason Wade and Ron Aniello

Copyright © 2000 Songs Of DreamWorks (BMI), G Chills Music (BMI), EMI Blackwood Music Inc. (BMI) and Aniello Music (BMI)
Worldwide Rights for Songs of Dreamworks and G Chills Music Administered by Cherry River Music Co.
Worldwide Rights for Aniello Music Controlled and Administered by EMI Blackwood Music Inc.
International Copyright Secured   All Rights Reserved

Bm　　Asus2　　Em　　Bm　　Asus2　　Em

___ bring me ___ back down? _   'Cause I've been liv - ing to see _____ my fears ___ as they___

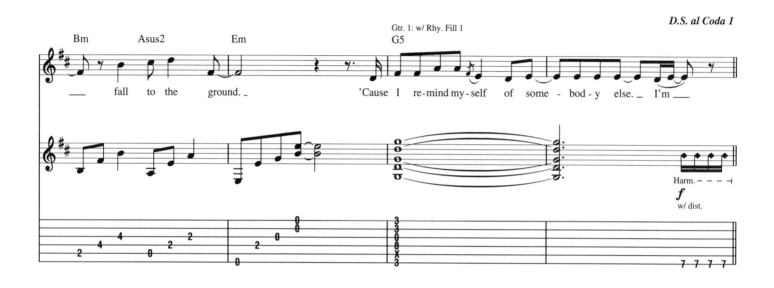

D.S. al Coda 1

Bm　　Asus2　　Em

Gtr. 1: w/ Rhy. Fill 1

G5

___ fall to the ground. _   'Cause I re-mind my-self of some - bod - y else. _ I'm ___

Harm. ----

f

w/ dist.

Coda 1

B5　　A5　　N.C.

want some of _____ my _____ own. _____

Gtr. 1

Gtr. 2

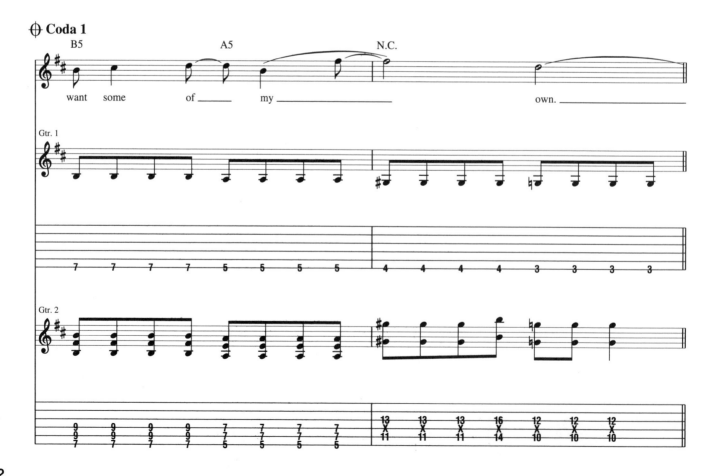

32

Interlude

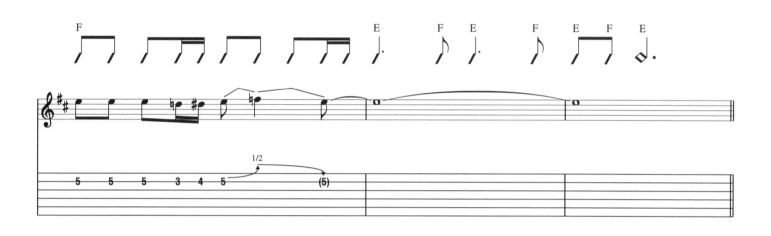

Verse

Gtr. 1: w/ Rhy. Fig. 1 (2 times)
Gtr. 3: w/ Riff A
Gtrs. 2 & 4 tacet

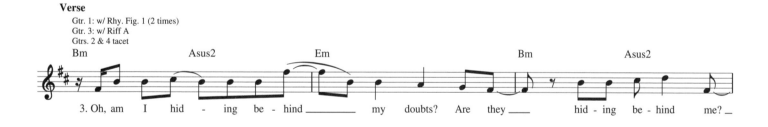

3. Oh, am I hid-ing be-hind _____ my doubts? Are they _____ hid-ing be-hind me? __

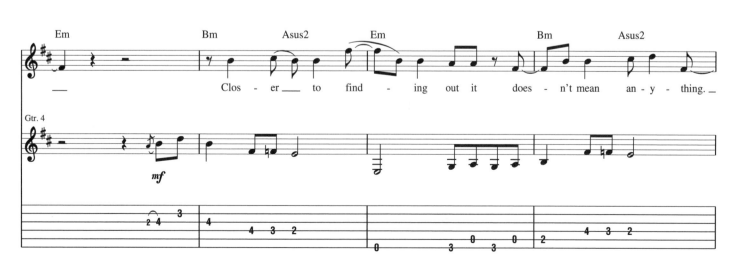

__ Clos-er __ to find - ing out it does-n't mean an-y-thing. __

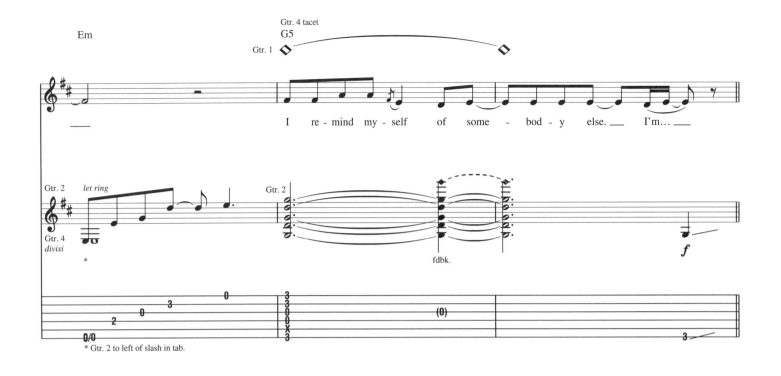

I re-mind my-self of some - bod - y else.___ I'm...___

* Gtr. 2 to left of slash in tab.

Interlude

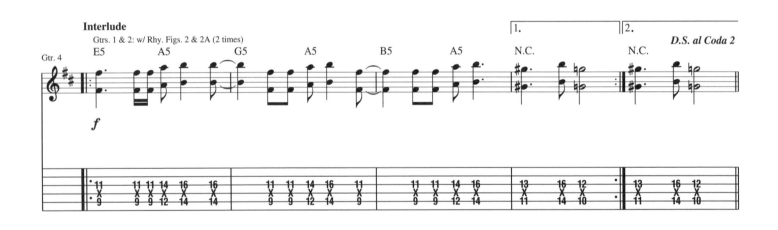

Coda 2

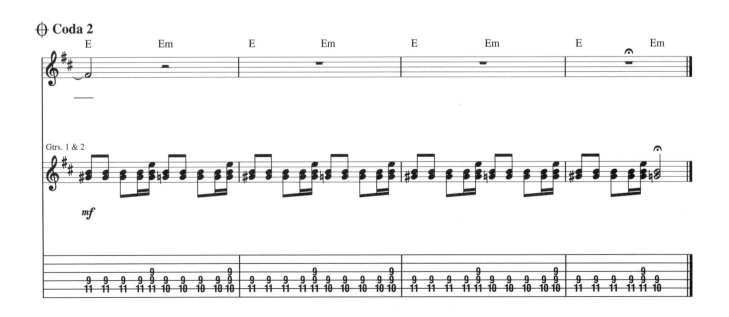

TRYING

Words and Music by
Jason Wade and Ron Aniello

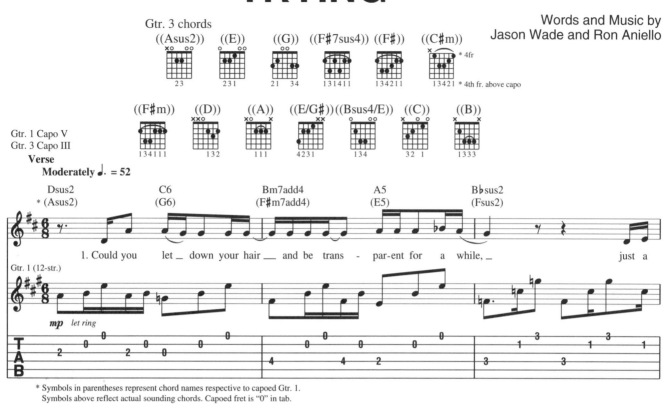

Copyright © 2000 Songs Of DreamWorks (BMI), G Chills Music (BMI), EMI Blackwood Music Inc. (BMI) and Aniello Music (BMI)
Worldwide Rights for Songs Of Dreamworks and G Chills Music Administered by Cherry River Music Co.
Worldwide Rights for Aniello Music Controlled and Administered by EMI Blackwood Music Inc.
International Copyright Secured   All Rights Reserved

all — want — to seem — like we've got it all ——— fig-ured out. Well,
work-ing on it. May-be I'll mas-ter this — art form some day.

End Rhy. Fig. 1

End Rhy. Fig. 1A

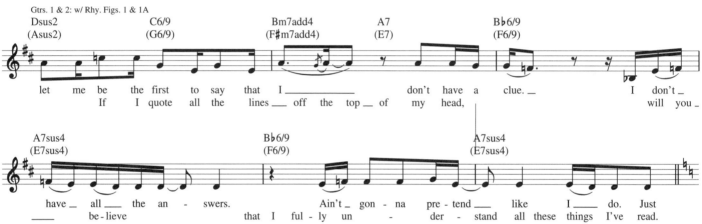

Gtrs. 1 & 2: w/ Rhy. Figs. 1 & 1A

let me be the first to say that I ——————— don't have a clue. — I don't —
If I quote all the lines — off the top — of my head,
will you —

have — all — the an - swers. Ain't — gon-na pre-tend — like I — do. Just
—— be-lieve that I ful-ly un - der-stand all these things I've read.

Chorus

*((Asus2))   ((E))   ((G))   ((F#7sus4))

Rhy. Fig. 2B   End Rhy. Fig. 2B

Gtr. 3

try - ing
I'm just try - ing   to find ——— my way.
(Try - ing   to find ——— my way.

Gtr. 1   Rhy. Fig. 2   End Rhy. Fig. 2

Gtr. 2   Rhy. Fig. 2A   End Rhy. Fig. 2A

* Symbols in double parentheses represent chord names respective to capoed Gtr. 3.

36

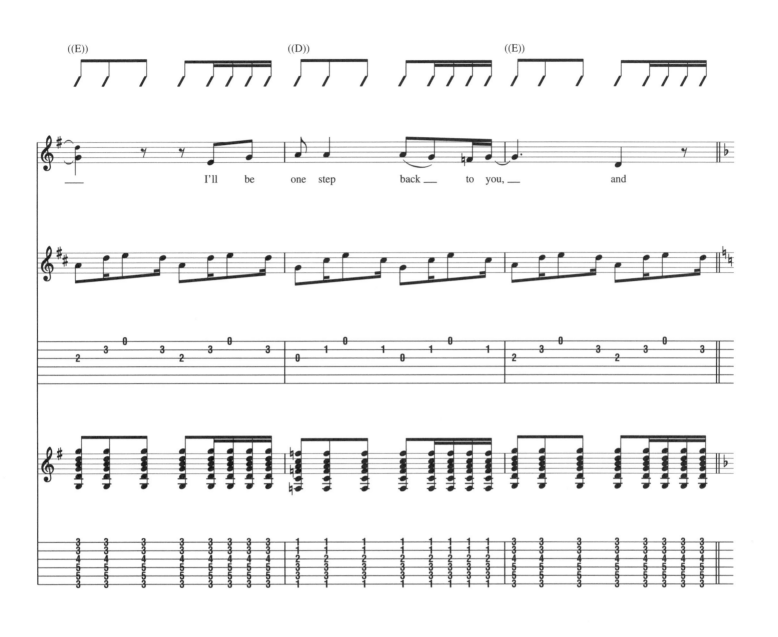

I'll be one step back to you, and

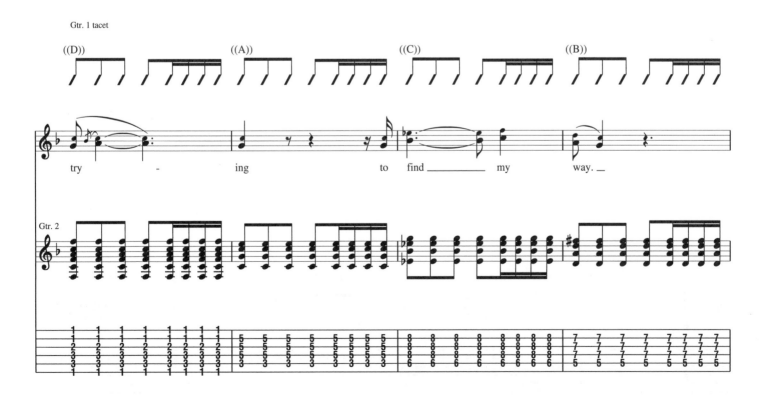

Gtr. 1 tacet

Gtr. 2

try - ing to find _____ my way. _

ONLY ONE

Words and Music by Jason Wade

Copyright © 2000 Songs Of DreamWorks (BMI) and G Chills Music (BMI)
Worldwide Rights for Songs Of Dreamworks and G Chills Music Administered by Cherry River Music Co.
International Copyright Secured   All Rights Reserved

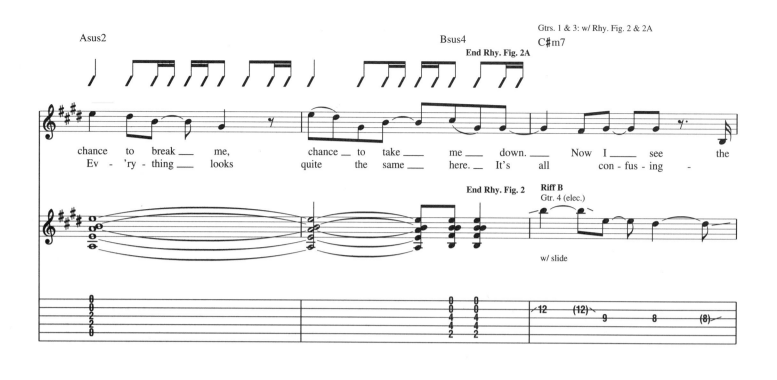

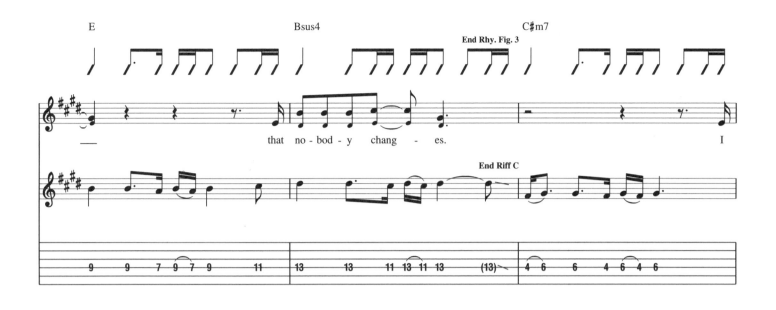

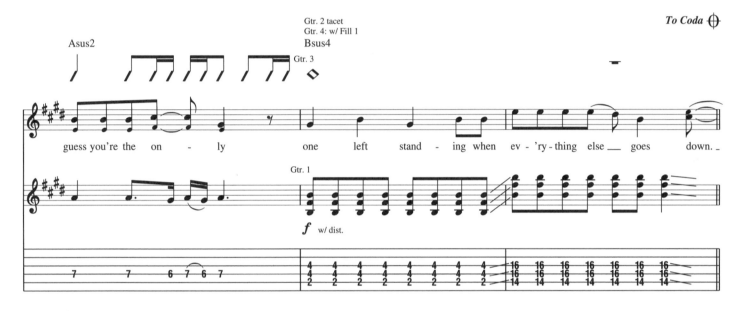

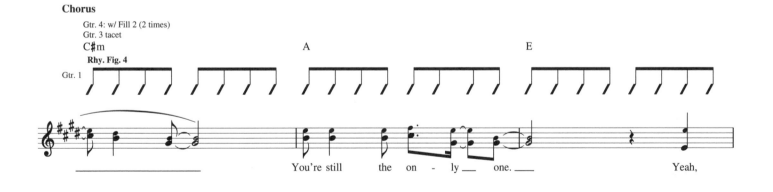

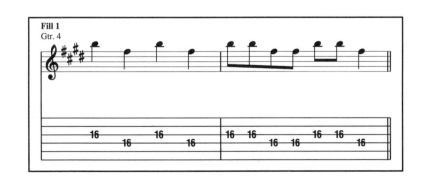
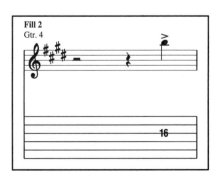

Interlude
Gtr. 1: w/ Rhy. Fig. 1 (2 times)
Gtr. 2: w/ Riff A

D.S. al Coda

you're still the on - ly ___ one. ___

Coda
Chorus
Gtr. 1: w/ Rhy. Fig. 4 (1 1/2 times)
Gtr. 2: w/ Riff C (2 times)
Gtr. 3 tacet
Gtr. 4: w/ Fill 2 (3 times)

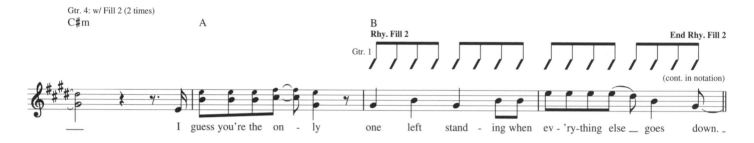

You're still the on - ly ___ one ___ who will nev - er change fac - es.

Gtr. 4: w/ Fill 2 (2 times)

I guess you're the on - ly one left stand - ing when ev - 'ry-thing else ___ goes down. ___

Bridge

Ah ba ba, ___ ah ba ba.

Gtr. 1: w/ Rhy. Fig. 5 (2 times)

Ooh, ah ba ba, ___ ooh, ah ba ba. ___ Ah ba ba, ___

Gtr. 1: w/ Rhy. Fill 2

ooh, ah ba ba, ___ yeah, ___ yeah, ___ yeah.

44

SIMON

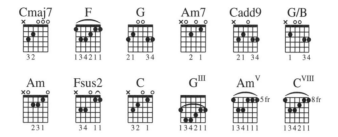

Words and Music by
Jason Wade and Ron Aniello

Tune down 1/2 step:
(low to high) E♭–A♭–D♭–G♭–B♭–E♭

Intro
Moderate Rock ♩ = 76

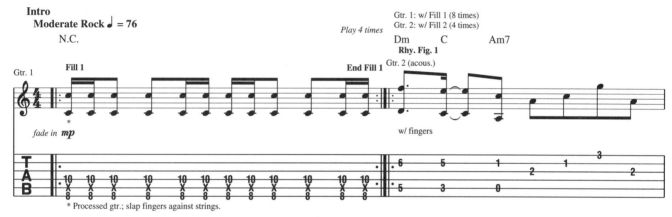

* Processed gtr.; slap fingers against strings.

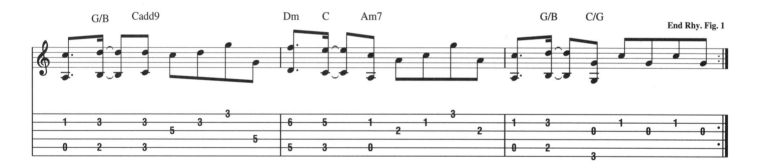

Verse

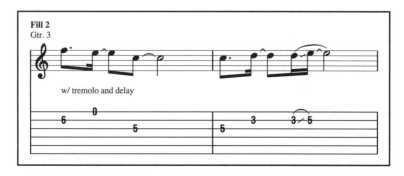

Copyright © 2000 Songs Of DreamWorks (BMI), G Chills Music (BMI), EMI Blackwood Music Inc. (BMI) and Aniello Music (BMI)
Worldwide Rights for Songs Of Dreamworks and G Chills Music Administered by Cherry River Music Co.
Worldwide Rights for Aniello Music Controlled and Administered by EMI Blackwood Music Inc.
International Copyright Secured   All Rights Reserved

Gtr. 3: w/ Riff A

fill - ment to ___ their lack ___ of strength ___ at your ___ ex - pense ___ left you with ___

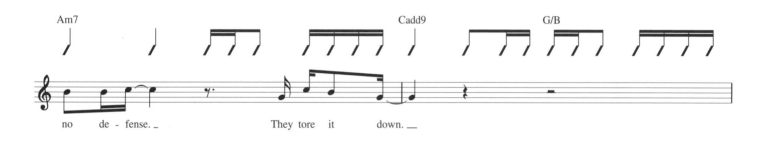

no de - fense. ___ They tore it down. ___

Rhy. Fill 1

End Rhy. Fill 1

And I have felt the same ___

Chorus

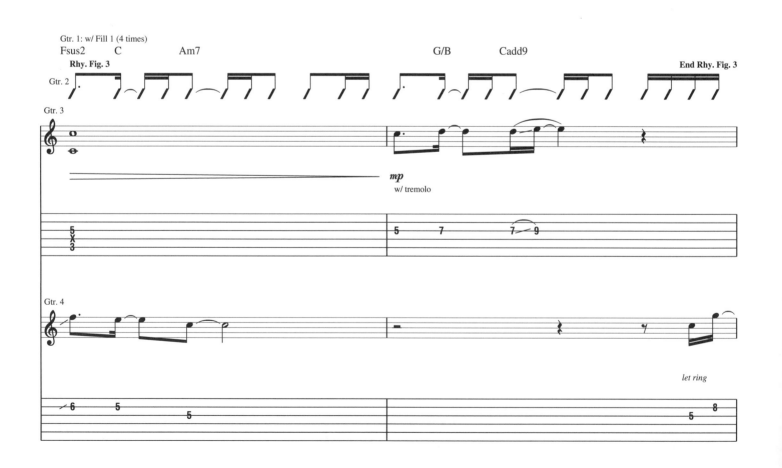

51

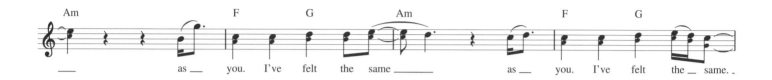

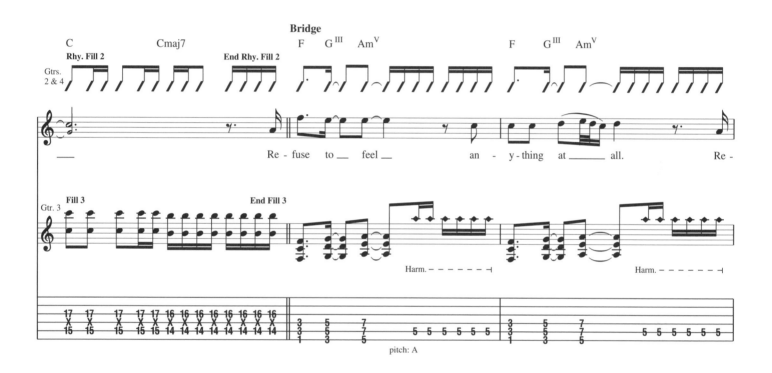

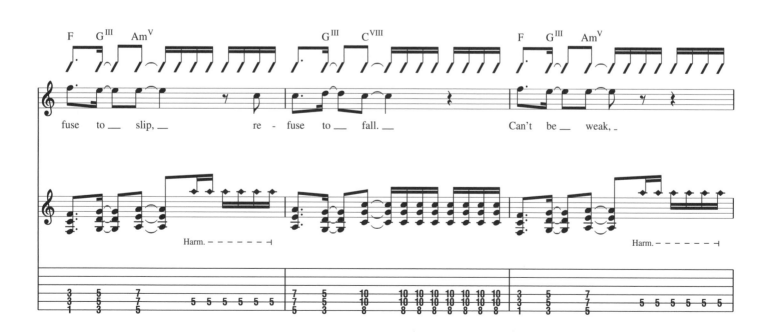

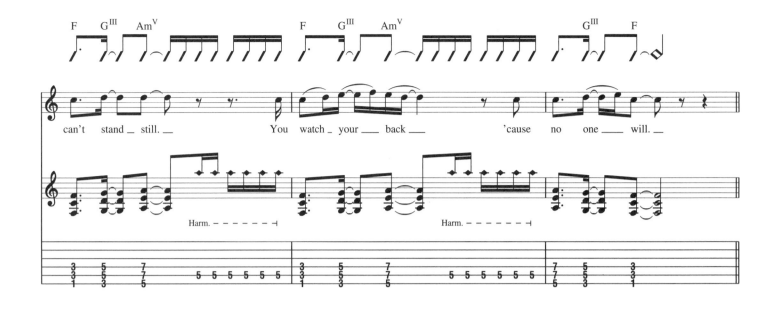

can't stand ___ still. ___ You watch ___ your ___ back ___ 'cause no one ___ will. ___

Pre-Chorus

Gtr. 1: w/ Fill 1 (8 times)
Gtr. 3: w/ Riff A (2 times)
Gtr. 4 tacet

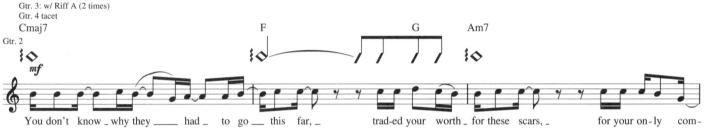

You don't know ___ why they ___ had ___ to go ___ this far, ___ trad-ed your worth ___ for these scars, ___ for your on-ly com-

- pan-y. Don't be-lieve ___ the lies ___ that they ___ have told ___ to you, ___ yeah, not one ___

Gtrs. 2 & 4: w/ Rhy. Fill 1

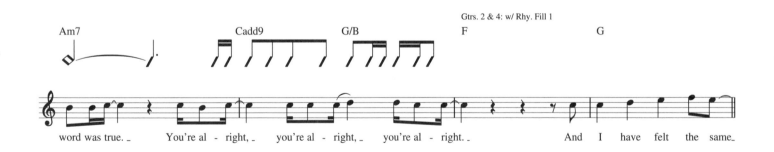

word was true. ___ You're al - right, ___ you're al - right, ___ you're al - right. ___ And I have felt the same ___

Chorus

Gtrs. 2 & 4: w/ Rhy. Figs. 2 & 2A (3 times)
Gtr. 3: w/ Riff B (3 times)

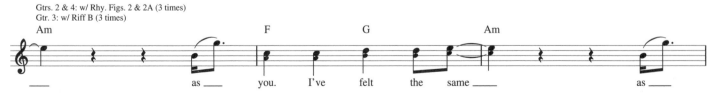

___ as ___ you. I've felt the same ___ as ___

F G Am *F/A G Gtrs. 2 & 4: w/ Rhy. Fill 2 / Gtr. 3: w/ Fill 3 / C Cmaj7

you. I've felt the same ___ as ___ you. I've felt the ___ same. ___ Oh.

* Bass plays A.

Outro

Gtrs. 2 & 4: w/ Rhy. Figs. 2 & 2A (last meas.)
Gtr. 3: w/ Riff B (3 times)

Gtrs. 1 & 2: w/ Rhy. Figs. 2 & 2A (2 1/2 times)

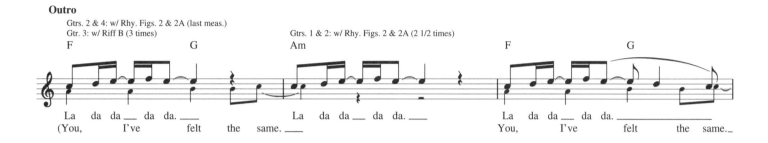

F G Am F G

La da da ___ da da. ___ La da da ___ da da. ___ La da da ___ da da. ___ You, I've felt the same. ___

(You, I've felt the same. ___)

Am F G Am

La da da ___ da da. ___ La da da ___ da da. ___ La da da ___ da da. ___ As

You, I've felt the same.)___

Gtr. 1: w/ Fill 1 (10 times)

Am G C

Gtr. 4

you. I've felt the ___ same. ___

Gtr. 3

Gtr. 2

mf

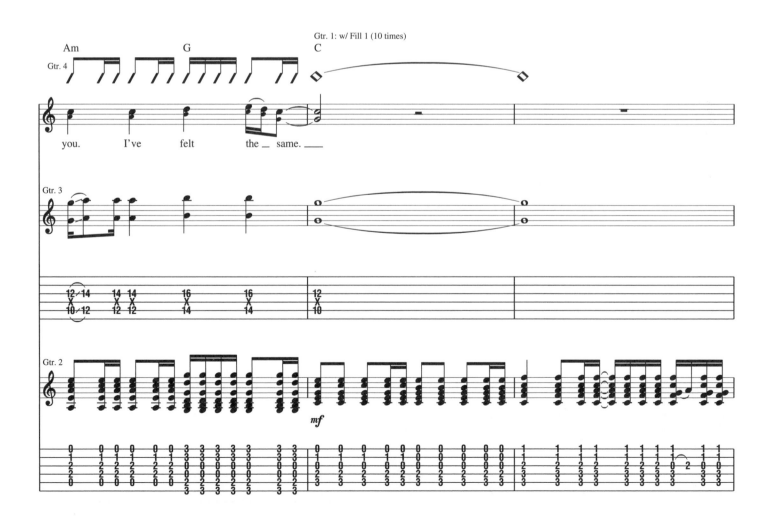

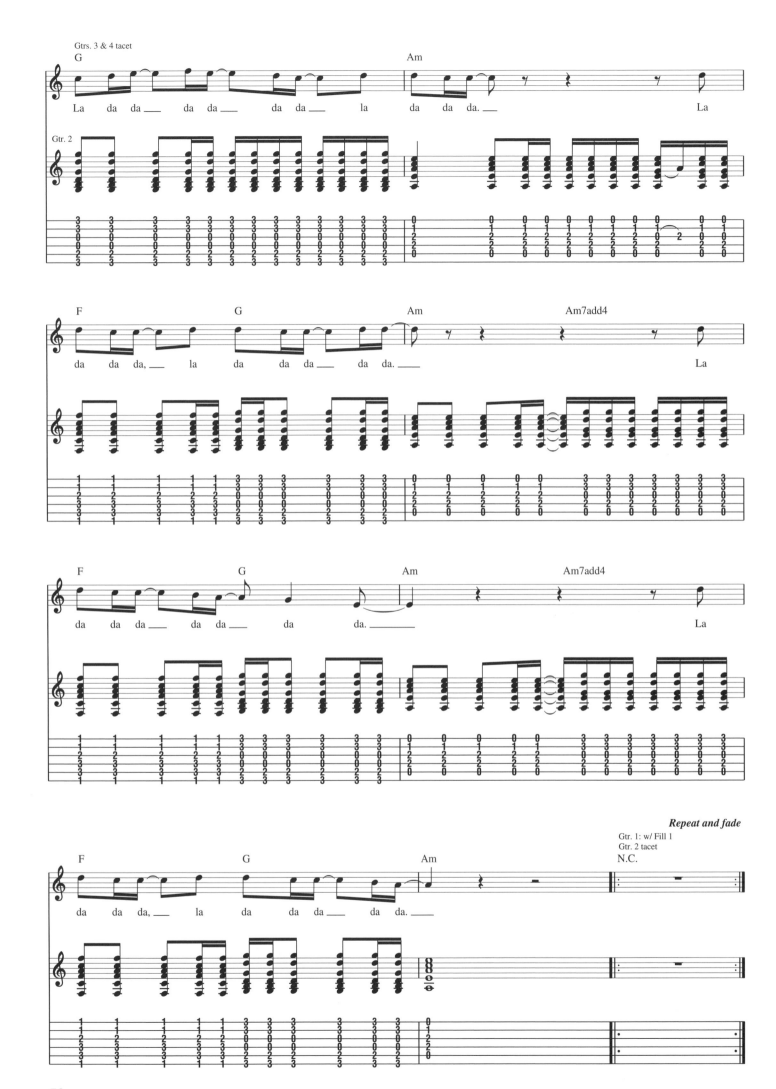

CLING AND CLATTER

Words and Music by
Jason Wade and Ron Aniello

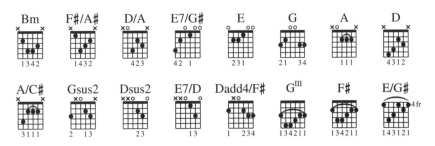

* With overdubbed gtr. fdbk. and noises created
  by plucking strings behind the nut (till Pre-Chorus).

Copyright © 2000 Songs Of DreamWorks (BMI), G Chills Music (BMI), EMI Blackwood Music Inc. (BMI) and Aniello Music (BMI)
Worldwide Rights for Songs Of DreamWorks and G Chills Music Administered by Cherry River Music Co.
Worldwide Rights for Aniello Music Controlled and Administered by EMI Blackwood Music Inc.
International Copyright Secured   All Rights Reserved

I find you, till you found me. And some-how I al-ways knew that you would. And

% **Pre-Chorus**

Gtr. 1: w/ Riff B

I am con-tem-plat-ing mat-ters. All this cling and clat-ter in my head.

Gtr. 2: w/ Rhy. Fig. 1
Gtr. 3: w/ Riff C

And what you said is ring-ing, ring-ing fast-er. And it's all good

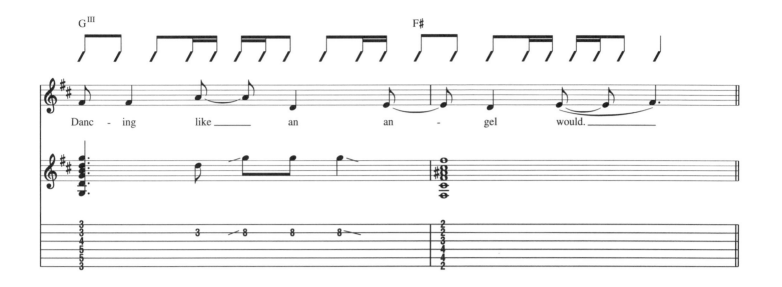

Danc - ing like _____ an an - gel would. _____

Interlude

* Gtr. 3: w/ Riff C (2 times)
Gtrs 1 & 2 tacet

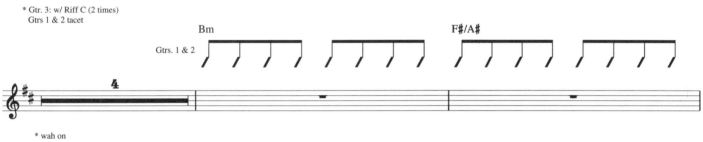

* wah on

D.S.S. al Coda 2

And it's all good _____

⊕ **Coda 2**

Gtrs. 1 & 2: w/ Rhy. Figs. 2 & 2A

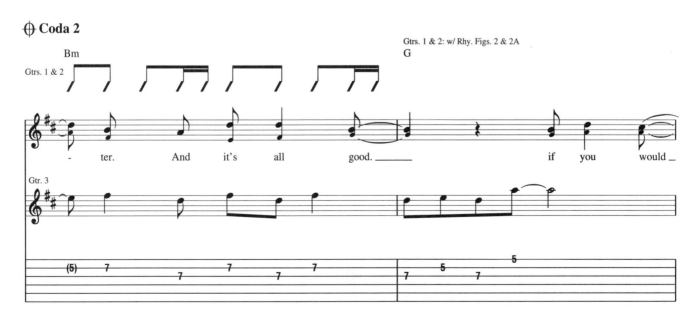

- ter. And it's all good. _____ if you would _____

BREATHING

Words and Music by
Jason Wade and Ron Aniello

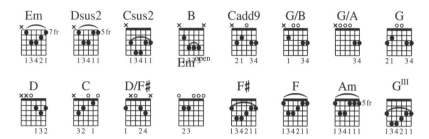

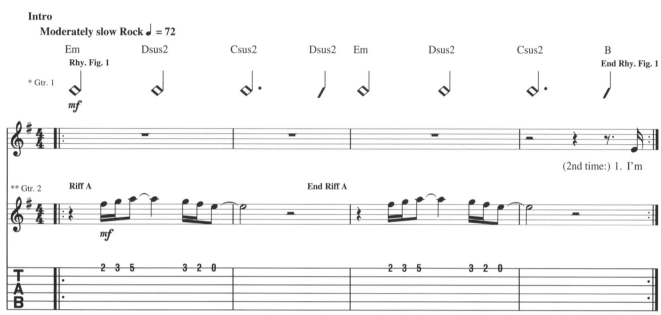

Tune down 1 step:
(low to high) D–G–C–F–A–D

Intro

Moderately slow Rock ♩ = 72

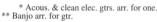

* Acous. & clean elec. gtrs. arr. for one.
** Banjo arr. for gtr.

Verse

Gtr. 2 tacet

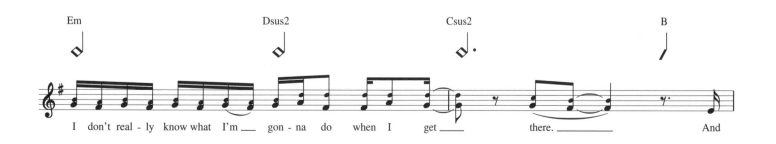

Copyright © 2000 Songs Of DreamWorks (BMI), G Chills Music (BMI), EMI Blackwood Music Inc. (BMI) and Aniello Music (BMI)
Worldwide Rights for Songs Of Dreamworks and G Chills Music Administered by Cherry River Music Co.
Worldwide Rights for Aniello Music Controlled and Administered by EMI Blackwood Music Inc.
International Copyright Secured   All Rights Reserved

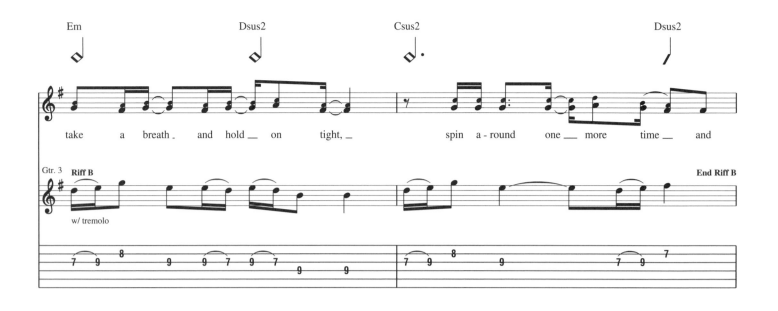

take a breath and hold _ on tight, _ spin a - round one _ more time _ and

grace - ful - ly ____ fall back in the arms of grace. _

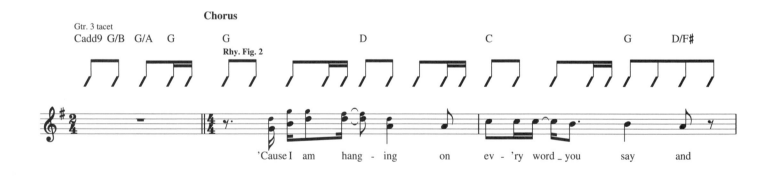

'Cause I am hang - ing on ev - 'ry word _ you say and

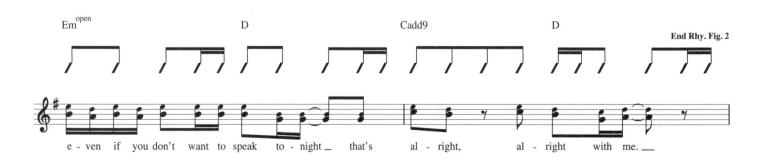

e - ven if you don't want to speak to - night _ that's al - right, al - right with me. _

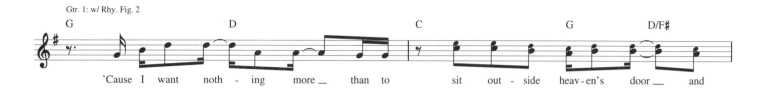

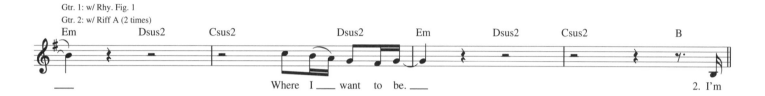

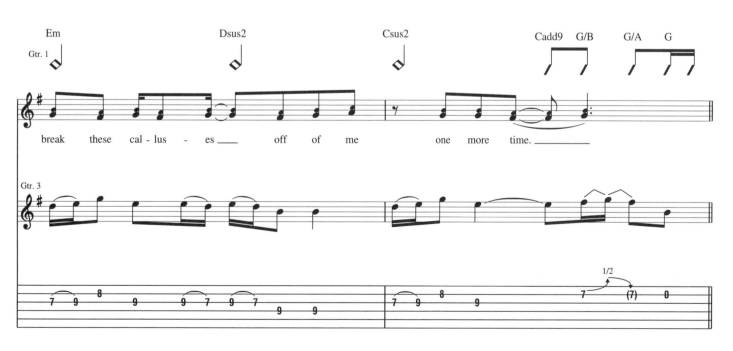

QUASIMODO

Words and Music by Jason Wade

Copyright © 2000 Songs Of DreamWorks (BMI) and G Chills Music (BMI)
Worldwide Rights for Songs Of Dreamworks and G Chills Music Administered by Cherry River Music Co.
International Copyright Secured   All Rights Reserved

off of my ___ back. ___ There it ___ goes. ___

Coda
Chorus
Gtrs. 1 & 2: w/ Rhy. Fig. 4
Gtr. 4: w/ Rhy. Fig. 4A
C G/B Am GIII
off of my shoul - ders. There goes the world
Gtr. 3 Riff C
F E F
Gtr. 3: w/ Riff B (1st 2 meas.)
Gtr. 4
off of my back. You can't change me, you can't break
End Riff C
Gtrs. 1 & 2
GIII C G/B
Gtr. 3: w/ Riff C
me. There goes the world off of my shoul -
Am GIII F GIII
- ders. There goes the world off of my back.

Bridge

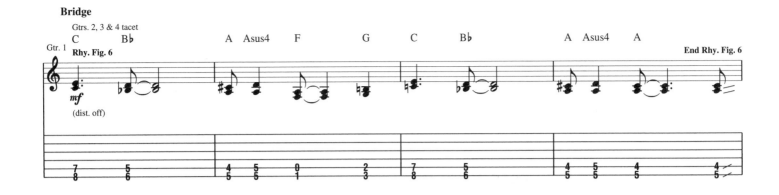

Have you ev-er felt like your on-ly com - fort was __ your cage? __ You're not a - lone. __

__ I have felt __ the same __ as you.

Have you ev-er felt like your se - crets give you __ a-way? You're not a - lone. __

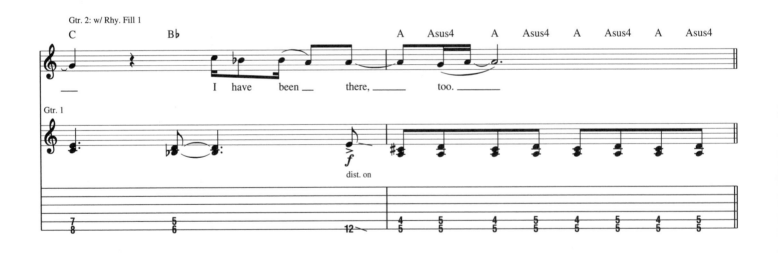

I have been __ there, __ too.

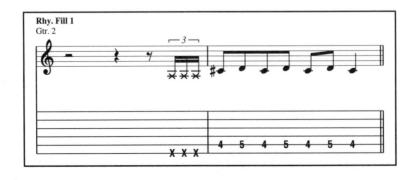

SOMEWHERE IN BETWEEN

Words and Music by Jason Wade

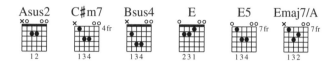

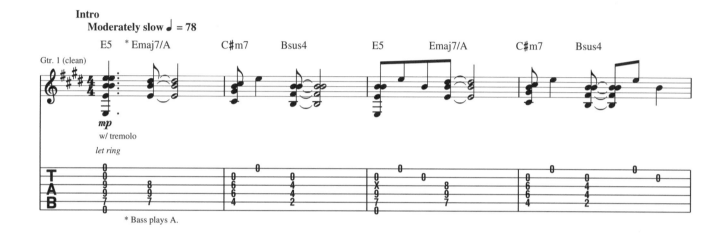

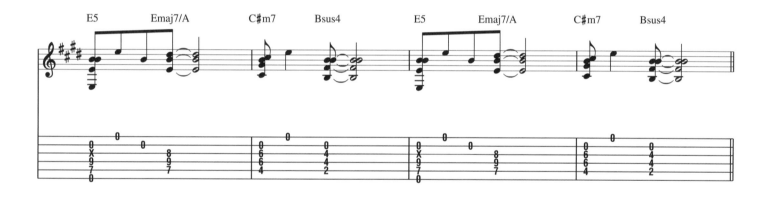

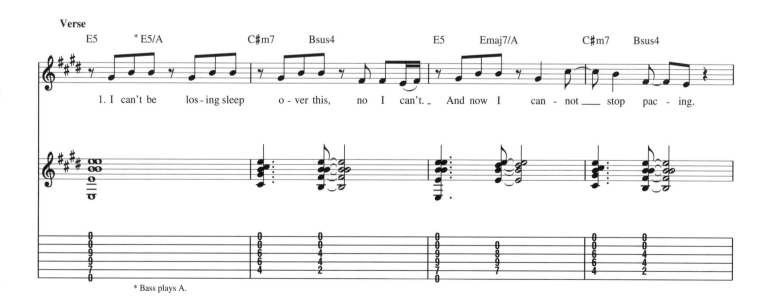

Copyright © 2000 Songs Of DreamWorks (BMI) and G Chills Music (BMI)
Worldwide Rights for Songs Of Dreamworks and G Chills Music Administered by Cherry River Music Co.
International Copyright Secured   All Rights Reserved

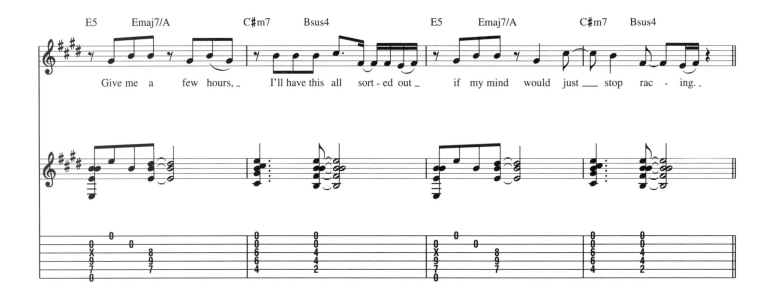

Give me a few hours, _ I'll have this all sort-ed out _ if my mind would just _ stop rac - ing. _

Pre-Chorus

Gtrs. 1 & 2: w/ Rhy. Fig. 1 (2 times)

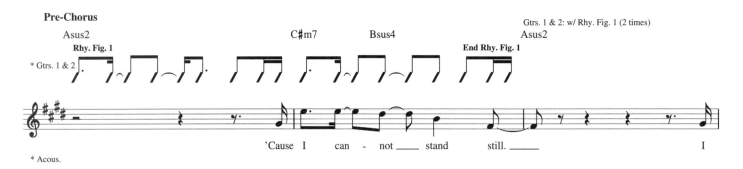

'Cause I can - not _ stand still. _____ I

can't be this _ un - stur - dy. This can - not _____ be hap -

Gtrs. 1 & 2: w/ Rhy. Fig. 1 (1st meas. only) (2 times)

Verse

- pen - ing. _ 2. This is o - ver my head

Gtrs. 1 & 2: w/ Rhy. Fig. 2 (3 times)

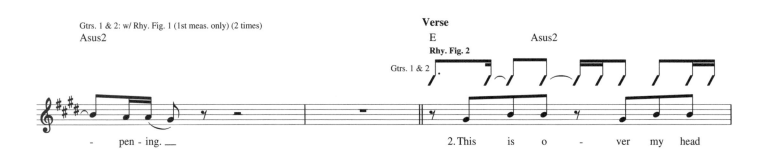

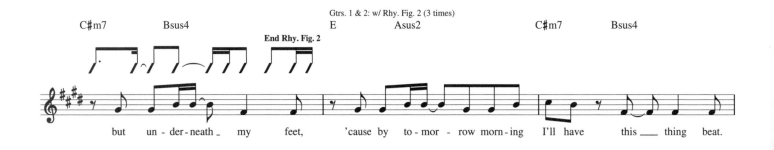

but un - der-neath _ my feet, 'cause by to - mor - row morn-ing I'll have this _ thing beat.

EVERYTHING

Words and Music by Jason Wade

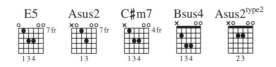

E5   Asus2   C#m7   Bsus4   Asus2 type2

Intro

Moderately ♩ = 92

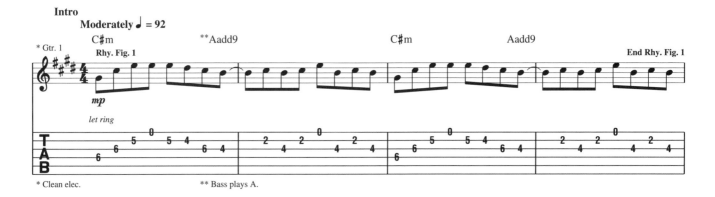

C#m   **Aadd9   C#m   Aadd9

* Gtr. 1   **Rhy. Fig. 1   End Rhy. Fig. 1

mp

let ring

* Clean elec.   ** Bass plays A.

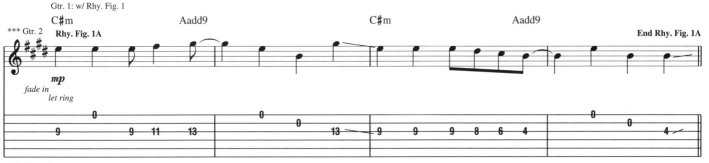

Gtr. 1: w/ Rhy. Fig. 1

C#m   Aadd9   C#m   Aadd9

*** Gtr. 2   Rhy. Fig. 1A   End Rhy. Fig. 1A

mp

fade in
let ring

*** Clean elec.

Verse

Gtrs. 1 & 2: w/ Rhy. Figs. 1 & 1A (both 4 times)

C#m   Aadd9   C#m   Aadd9   C#m   Aadd9

1. Find _ me here _   and speak _ to _ me. _   I want _ to feel _

C#m   Aadd9   C#m   Aadd9

_ you.   I need _ to hear _ you. _   You are _ the light _

C#m   Aadd9   C#m   Aadd9

_   that's lead - ing _ me _   to _ the place _

Interlude

† Gtrs. 1 & 3: w/ Rhy. Fig. 1
Gtr. 2: w/ Rhy. Fig. 1A

C#m   Aadd9   C#m   Aadd9   C#m   Aadd9

where I _ find _ peace _   a - gain. _

† Gtr. 3: 12-str. acous.

Copyright © 2000 Songs Of DreamWorks (BMI) and G Chills Music (BMI)
Worldwide Rights for Songs Of Dreamworks and G Chills Music Administered by Cherry River Music Co.
International Copyright Secured   All Rights Reserved

Verse

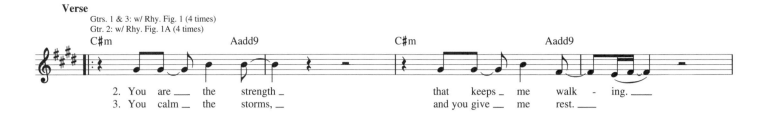

2. You are ___ the strength ___ that keeps ___ me walk - ing. ___
3. You calm ___ the storms, ___ and you give ___ me rest. ___

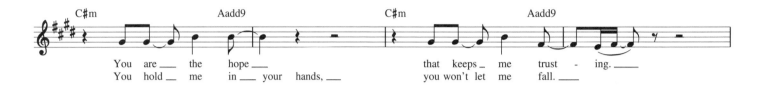

You are ___ the hope ___ that keeps ___ me trust - ing. ___
You hold ___ me in ___ your hands, ___ you won't let me fall. ___

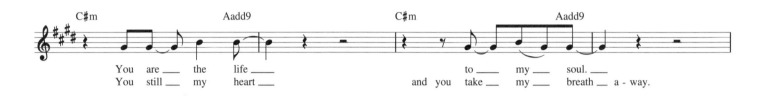

You are ___ the life ___ to ___ my ___ soul. ___
You still ___ my heart ___ and you take ___ my ___ breath a - way.

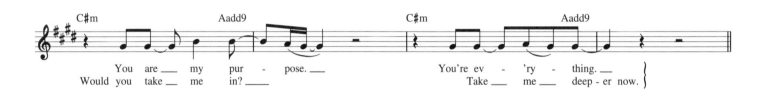

You are ___ my pur - pose. ___ You're ev - 'ry - thing. ___
Would you take ___ me in? ___ Take ___ me ___ deep - er now.

Chorus

And how ___ can I ___ stand here with you ___ and not be moved ___ by you? ___

82

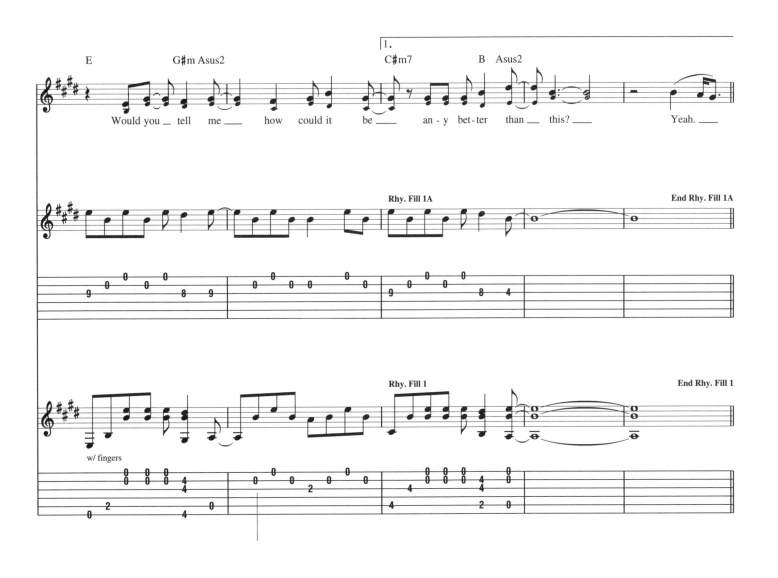

E   G#m Asus2   C#m7   B Asus2

Would you __ tell me __ how could it be __ an-y bet-ter than __ this? __ Yeah. __

Rhy. Fill 1A   End Rhy. Fill 1A

Rhy. Fill 1   End Rhy. Fill 1

w/ fingers

Interlude
Gtrs. 1 & 3: w/ Rhy. Fig. 1
Gtr. 2: w/ Rhy. Fig. 1A
C#m   Aadd9   C#m   Aadd9

Gtrs. 1 & 3: w/ Rhy. Fig. 2 (last 2 meas. only)
Gtr. 2: w/ Rhy. Fig. 2A (last 2 meas. only)
C#m7   B   Asus2

__ an - y bet - ter than __ this? _____

Gtrs. 1 & 3: w/ Rhy. Fig. 2 (1 1/2 times)
Gtr. 2: w/ Rhy. Fig. 2A (1 1/2 times)
E   G#m Asus2   C#m7   B   Asus2

And how __ can I _____ stand here with you ___ and not be moved __ by you? __

Gtrs. 1 & 3: w/ Rhy. Fill 1
Gtr. 2: w/ Rhy. Fill 1A
E   G#m Asus2   C#m7   B   Asus2

Would you __ tell me __ how could it be ___ an-y-bet-ter than __ this? __ 'Cause you're all I want, __

Bridge

* Two gtrs. w/ dist. arr. for one.

    ** Chord symbols reflect implied harmony.

Chorus

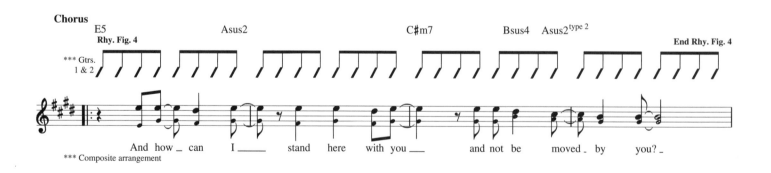

*** Composite arrangement

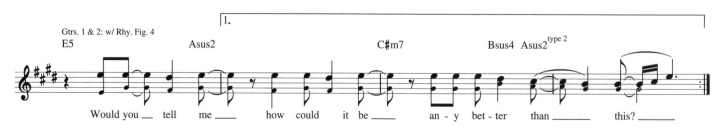

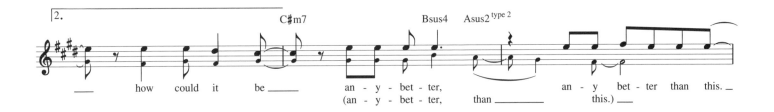

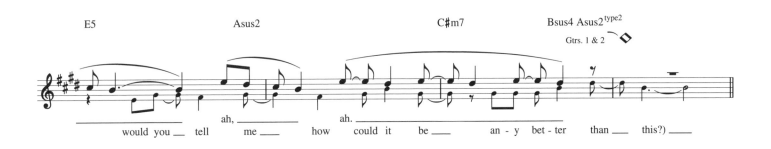

Guitar Notation Legend

Guitar Music can be notated three different ways: on a *musical staff*, in *tablature*, and in *rhythm slashes*.

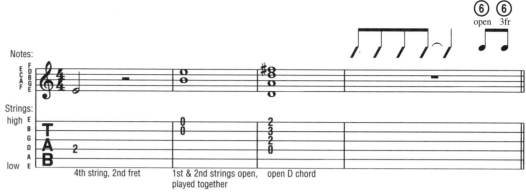

RHYTHM SLASHES are written above the staff. Strum chords in the rhythm indicated. Use the chord diagrams found at the top of the first page of the transcription for the appropriate chord voicings. Round noteheads indicate single notes.

THE MUSICAL STAFF shows pitches and rhythms and is divided by bar lines into measures. Pitches are named after the first seven letters of the alphabet.

TABLATURE graphically represents the guitar fingerboard. Each horizontal line represents a string, and each number represents a fret.

4th string, 2nd fret   1st & 2nd strings open, played together   open D chord

---

HALF-STEP BEND: Strike the note and bend up 1/2 step.

WHOLE-STEP BEND: Strike the note and bend up one step.

GRACE NOTE BEND: Strike the note and immediately bend up as indicated.

SLIGHT (MICROTONE) BEND: Strike the note and bend up 1/4 step.

BEND AND RELEASE: Strike the note and bend up as indicated, then release back to the original note. Only the first note is struck.

PRE-BEND: Bend the note as indicated, then strike it.

VIBRATO: The string is vibrated by rapidly bending and releasing the note with the fretting hand.

WIDE VIBRATO: The pitch is varied to a greater degree by vibrating with the fretting hand.

HAMMER-ON: Strike the first (lower) note with one finger, then sound the higher note (on the same string) with another finger by fretting it without picking.

PULL-OFF: Place both fingers on the notes to be sounded. Strike the first note and without picking, pull the finger off to sound the second (lower) note.

LEGATO SLIDE: Strike the first note and then slide the same fret-hand finger up or down to the second note. The second note is not struck.

SHIFT SLIDE: Same as legato slide, except the second note is struck.

TRILL: Very rapidly alternate between the notes indicated by continuously hammering on and pulling off.

TAPPING: Hammer ("tap") the fret indicated with the pick-hand index or middle finger and pull off to the note fretted by the fret hand.

NATURAL HARMONIC: Strike the note while the fret-hand lightly touches the string directly over the fret indicated.

PINCH HARMONIC: The note is fretted normally and a harmonic is produced by adding the edge of the thumb or the tip of the index finger of the pick hand to the normal pick attack.

PICK SCRAPE: The edge of the pick is rubbed down (or up) the string, producing a scratchy sound.

MUFFLED STRINGS: A percussive sound is produced by laying the fret hand across the string(s) without depressing, and striking them with the pick hand.

PALM MUTING: The note is partially muted by the pick hand lightly touching the string(s) just before the bridge.

RAKE: Drag the pick across the strings indicated with a single motion.

TREMOLO PICKING: The note is picked as rapidly and continuously as possible.

VIBRATO BAR DIVE AND RETURN: The pitch of the note or chord is dropped a specified number of steps (in rhythm) then returned to the original pitch.

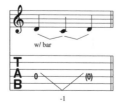

VIBRATO BAR SCOOP: Depress the bar just before striking the note, then quickly release the bar.

VIBRATO BAR DIP: Strike the note and then immediately drop a specified number of steps, then release back to the original pitch.

THE *HOTTEST* TAB SONGBOOKS AVAILABLE FOR GUITAR & BASS!

PLAY IT LIKE IT IS GUITAR WITH TABLATURE
NOTE-FOR-NOTE TRANSCRIPTIONS

PLAY IT LIKE IT IS BASS WITH TABLATURE
NOTE-FOR-NOTE TRANSCRIPTIONS

from  CHERRY LANE MUSIC COMPANY

Guitar Transcriptions

02500009	Bush – Best of	$19.95
02501272	Bush – 16 Stone	$21.95
02501288	Bush – Razorblade Suitcase	$21.95
02500193	Bush – The Science of Things	$19.95
02500098	Coal Chamber	$19.95
02500174	Coal Chamber – Chamber Music	$19.95
02501257	Faith No More – King for a Day/ Fool for a Lifetime	$19.95
02507093	Faith No More – The Real Thing	$19.95
02501262	Fates Warning – Best of	$21.95
02500132	Evolution of Fear Factory	$19.95
02501242	Guns N' Roses – Anthology	$24.95
02506953	Guns N' Roses – Appetite for Destruction	$22.95
02501286	Guns N' Roses Complete, Volume 1	$24.95
02501287	Guns N' Roses Complete, Volume 2	$24.95
02506211	Guns N' Roses – 5 of the Best, Vol. 1	$12.95
02506975	Guns N' Roses – GN'R Lies	$19.95
02501193	Guns N' Roses – Use Your Illusion I	$24.95
02501194	Guns N' Roses – Use Your Illusion II	$24.95
02500007	Hole – Celebrity Skin	$19.95
02501260	Hole – Live Through This	$19.95
02500012	Lenny Kravitz – 5	$16.95
02500024	Best of Lenny Kravitz	$19.95
02501270	Lenny Kravitz – Circus	$19.95
02501283	Los Lobos – Colossal Head	$19.95
02501259	Machine Head – Burn My Eyes	$19.95
02500173	Machine Head – The Burning Red	$19.95
02501357	Dave Matthews Band – Before These Crowded Streets	$19.95
02501279	Dave Matthews Band – Crash	$19.95
02501266	Dave Matthews Band – Under the Table and Dreaming	$19.95
02500131	Dave Matthews/Tim Reynolds – Live at Luther College	$19.95
02501195	Metallica – Metallica	$22.95
02506965	Metallica – ...And Justice for All	$22.95
02500070	Metallica – Garage Inc.	$24.95
02507018	Metallica – Kill 'Em All	$19.95
02501232	Metallica – Live: Binge & Purge	$19.95
02501275	Metallica – Load	$24.95
02507920	Metallica – Master of Puppets	$19.95
02501297	Metallica – Reload	$24.95
02507019	Metallica – Ride the Lightning	$19.95
02506210	Metallica – 5 of the Best/Vol. 1	$12.95
02506235	Metallica – 5 of the Best/Vol. 2	$12.95
02501189	Mr. Big – Lean Into It	$19.95
02501353	Best of Steve Morse	$19.95
02501277	Ozzy Osbourne – Diary of a Madman	$19.95
02509973	Ozzy Osbourne – Songbook	$24.95
02507904	Ozzy Osbourne/Randy Rhoads Tribute	$22.95
02500194	Powerman 5000 – Tonight the Stars Revolt!	$17.95
02500025	Primus Anthology – A-N (Guitar/Bass)	$19.95
02500091	Primus Anthology – O-Z (Guitar/Bass)	$19.95
02501255	Best of Joe Satriani	$19.95
02501268	Joe Satriani	$22.95
02501299	Joe Satriani – Crystal Planet	$24.95
02501205	Joe Satriani – The Extremist	$22.95
02506236	Joe Satriani – 5 of the Best/Vol. 2	$12.95
02507029	Joe Satriani – Flying in a Blue Dream	$22.95
02507074	Joe Satriani – Not of This Earth	$19.95
02506959	Joe Satriani – Surfing with the Alien	$19.95
02501226	Joe Satriani – Time Machine 1	$19.95
02501227	Joe Satriani – Time Machine 2	$19.95
02500088	Sepultura – Against	$19.95
02501239	Sepultura – Arise	$19.95
02501240	Sepultura – Beneath the Remains	$19.95
02501238	Sepultura – Chaos A.D.	$19.95
02501271	Sepultura – Roots	$19.95
02501241	Sepultura – Schizophrenia	$19.95
02500188	Best of the Brian Setzer Orchestra	$19.95
02500177	Sevendust	$19.95
02500176	Sevendust – Home	$19.95
02501246	Slayer – Decade of Aggression	$19.95
02501358	Slayer – Diabolus in Musica	$21.95
02501244	Slayer – Divine Intervention	$19.95
02501229	Slayer – Haunting the Chapel	$14.95
02501167	Slayer – Hell Awaits	$19.95
02501264	Primal Slayer for Guitar	$19.95
02501215	Slayer – Reign in Blood	$19.95
02501179	Slayer – Seasons in the Abyss	$19.95
02501282	Slayer – Undisputed Attitude	$19.95
02500090	Soulfly	$19.95
02501250	Best of Soundgarden	$19.95
02501198	Soundgarden – Badmotorfinger	$19.95
02501230	Soundgarden – Superunknown	$19.95
02500167	Best of Steely Dan for Guitar	$19.95
02500168	Steely Dan's Greatest Songs	$19.95
02501263	Tesla – Time's Making Changes	$19.95
02501251	Type O Negative – Bloody Kisses	$19.95
02501154	Ugly Kid Joe – America's Least Wanted	$19.95
02506972	Steve Vai – Songbook	$19.95
02500104	WWF: The Music, Vol. 3	$19.95

Bass Transcriptions

02500008	Best of Bush	$16.95
02505920	Bush – 16 Stone	$19.95
02500114	Guitar Presents the Great Bassists	$16.95
02506966	Guns N' Roses – Appetite for Destruction	$19.95
02500013	Best of The Dave Matthews Band	$16.95
02505911	Metallica – Metallica	$19.95
02506982	Metallica – ...And Justice for All	$19.95
02500075	Metallica – Garage, Inc.	$24.95
02507039	Metallica – Kill 'Em All	$19.95
02505919	Metallica – Load	$19.95
02506961	Metallica – Master of Puppets	$19.95
02505926	Metallica – Reload	$21.95
02507040	Metallica – Ride the Lightning	$17.95
02505925	Ozzy Osbourne – Diary of a Madman	$17.95
02500025	Primus Anthology – A-N (Guitar/Bass)	$19.95
02500091	Primus Anthology – O-Z (Guitar/Bass)	$19.95
02505918	Best of Sepultura for Bass	$18.95
02505924	Primal Slayer for Bass	$16.95
02505917	Best of Soundgarden	$16.95

Prices, contents and availability subject to change without notice.

OR WRITE TO:

HAL•LEONARD® CORPORATION
7777 W. BLUEMOUND RD. P.O. BOX 13819 MILWAUKEE, WI 53213

0800

Guitar one

The Magazine You Can Play

Visit the Guitar One web site at www.guitarone.com

CHERRY LANE
MUSIC COMPANY

GuitarOne Presents · The Best Bass Lines

INCLUDES **TAB**

Get the low-down on the low-end sounds from 24 super songs, straight from the pages of *GuitarOne* magazine! Includes note-for-note bass transcriptions with tab for: Badge • Bohemian Rhapsody • Celebrity Skin • Crash into Me • Crazy Train • Everything Zen • Glycerine • Jerry Was a Race Car Driver • Money • November Rain • Smoke on the Water • Suffragette City • Sweet Child O' Mine • Violet • What Would You Say • You're My Flavor • and more.

_____02500311 Play-It-Like-It-Is Bass $14.95

GuitarOne Presents · Blues Licks for Guitar · *by Chris Amelar*

A great guide to blues improvisation that will fit in your guitar case! This book will help you develop a strong blues vocabulary by teaching many of the licks and phrases essential to playing blues solos. Also examines scales used in blues improv, and techniques like bending and vibrato. Includes an intro by guitar pro Chris Amelar, and a complete 12-bar blues solo at the end of the book. 4¼" x 12"

_____02500118...$5.95

GuitarOne Presents · Blues Rockers

INCLUDES **TAB**

12 rockin' blues favorites, including: Changes • I Can't Quit You Baby • Jingo (Jin-Go-Lo-Ba) • Ramblin' Man • Smoking Gun • Steppin' Out • Tightrope • and more.

_____02500264 Play-It-Like-It-Is Guitar $14.95

GuitarOne Presents · Legends of Lead Guitar

The Best of Interviews: 1995-2000

Who can explain the extensive thought processes and flights of fancy by which a virtuoso guitarist makes a metal, wood & wire contraption sing, snarl, whisper or weep? None but the artist. Hence this book. *Legends of Lead Guitar* is a fascinating compilation of *GuitarOne* magazine interviews with today's greatest lead guitarists – and your backstage pass to the art of the rock'n'roll axe! From deeply rooted blues giants to the most fearless pioneer, legendary players reveal how they achieve their extraordinary craft. Artists featured include: AC/DC • Aerosmith • Jeff Beck • Black Crowes • Bush • Coal Chamber • Collective Soul • Creed • Deftones • Ani DiFranco • Kevin Eubanks • Foo Fighters • Goo Goo Dolls • Buddy Guy • Eric Johnson • Kid Rock • B.B. King • Kiss • Korn • Lenny Kravitz • Limp Bizkit • Metallica • Dave Navarro • Jimmy Page • Pantera • Les Paul • Rage Against the Machine • Red Hot Chili Peppers • Carlos Santana • Kenny Wayne Shepherd • Andy Summers • Third Eye Blind • Steve Vai • Eddie Van Halen • and more!

_____02500329 ....$19.95

GuitarOne Presents · Lesson Lab

This exceptional book/CD pack features more than 20 in-depth lessons from the pages of *GuitarOne* magazine's most popular department. Tackle a variety of pertinent music- and guitar-related subjects, such as scales, chords, theory, guitar technique, songwriting, and much more!

_____02500330 Book/CD Pack...$19.95

GuitarOne Presents · Noise and Feedback

_____02500328 ....$16.95

GuitarOne Presents · Rock Legends

INCLUDES **TAB**

Transcriptions with tab for 21 rock classics from some of the greatest guitarists ever! Includes: All Along the Watchtower (Hendrix) • Badge (Cream) • Crazy on You (Heart) • Crazy Train (Osbourne) • Flying in a Blue Dream (Satriani) • Hide Away (Clapton) • Hot Blooded (Foreigner) • Sweet Child O' Mine (Guns N' Roses) • Telephone Song (Stevie Ray Vaughan) • You Really Got Me (Van Halen) • and more.

_____02500262 Play-It-Like-It-Is Guitar...$14.95

GuitarOne Presents · Signature Songs

INCLUDES **TAB**

This cool collection features 21 artists and note-for-note transcriptions of the hit songs that remind us of them! Includes: Aerosmith, "Walk This Way" • Cream, "Sunshine of Your Love" • Guns N' Roses, "Welcome to the Jungle" • Dave Matthews Band, "What Would You Say" • Ozzy Osbourne, "Crazy Train" • Santana, "Smooth" • Van Halen, "You Really Got Me" • The Who, "My Generation" • and more!

_____02500303 Play-It-Like-It-Is Guitar...$16.95

GuitarOne Presents · Studio City · *by Carl Verheyen*

Professional guitarist Carl Verheyen chronicles his career as one of L.A.'s top-call session players in this complete collection of his Studio City columns from *Guitar* magazine. He draws on his vast experience to advise guitarists how to: exercise studio etiquette and act professionally • acquire, assemble and set up gear for sessions • use the tricks of the trade to become a studio hero • get repeat callbacks • and much more. This is the handbook for recording guitarists who want a career as a professional studio player!

_____02500195 ....$9.95

Prices, contents, and availability subject to change without notice.

EXCLUSIVELY DISTRIBUTED BY

HAL•LEONARD® CORPORATION

7777 W. BLUEMOUND RD. P.O. BOX 13819 MILWAUKEE, WI 53213

Visit Cherry Lane Online at **www.cherrylane.com**